Kids' Silliest
Knock-knocks

By **Jacqueline Horsfall**
Illustrated by **Buck Jones**

Sterling Publishing Co., Inc.
New York

For Bill, who always keeps me laughing

Library of Congress Cataloging-in-Publication Data Available

10 9 8 7 6 5 4 3

Published by Sterling Publishing Co., Inc.
387 Park Avenue South, New York, NY 10016
© 2004 by Jacqueline Horsfall
Distributed in Canada by Sterling Publishing
℅ Canadian Manda Group, 165 Dufferin Street,
Toronto, Ontario, Canada M6K 3H6
Distributed in the United Kingdom by GMC Distribution Services,
Castle Place, 166 High Street, Lewes, East Sussex, England BN7 1XU
Distributed in Australia by Capricorn Link (Australia) Pty. Ltd.
P.O. Box 704, Windsor, NSW 2756, Australia

Sterling ISBN-13: 978-1-4027-1135-0 Hardcover
        ISBN-10: 1-4027-1135-2
        ISBN-13: 978-1-4027-2221-9 Paperback
        ISBN-10: 1-4027-2221-4

For information about custom editions, special sales, premium
and corporate purchases, please contact Sterling Special Sales
Department at 800-805-5489 or specialsales@sterlingpub.com

Knock-knock.
Who's there?
Aaron.
Aaron who?
Aaron my tires, gas in my tank...so let's go!

Knock-knock.
Who's there?
Abbie.
Abbie who?
Abbie stung my big toe!

3

Knock-knock.
Who's there?
Ada.
Ada who?
Ada hamburger, yum-yum...want one?

Knock-knock.
Who's there?
Aisle.
Aisle who?
Aisle never tell your secret.

Knock-knock.
Who's there?
Alaska.
Alaska who?
Alaska, but I don't think Mom will let me bungee jump.

Knock-knock.
Who's there?
Aleta.
Aleta who?
Aleta whole pizza by myself.

Knock-knock.
Who's there?
Allison.
Allison who?
Allison Wonderland.

        Knock-knock.
        Who's there?
        Althea.
        Althea who?
        Althea when I get out of
        detention.

Knock-knock.
Who's there?
Ammonia.
Ammonia who?
Ammonia little kid, so I can't reach the doorbell.

        Knock-knock.
        Who's there?
        Andrew.
        Andrew who?
        Andrew on the walls, and was her
        mother mad!

Knock-knock.
Who's there?
Andy.
Andy who?
Andy huffed and he puffed and he blew my
house down!

Knock-knock.
Who's there?
Anita.
Anita who?
Anita shower, now!

Knock-knock.
Who's there?
Annapolis.
Annapolis who?
Annapolis is what you eat each
day to keep the doctor away.

Knock-knock.
Who's there?
Anton.
Anton who?
Anton your potato salad. Don't worry, it won't
eat much.

Knock-knock.
Who's there?
Appeal.
Appeal who?
Appeal is what covers a banana.

Knock-knock.
Who's there?
Archibald.
Archibald who?
Archibald, but he's buying a wig tomorrow.

Knock-knock.
Who's there?
Bacon.
Bacon who?
Bacon a chocolate cake for your birthday.

> Knock-knock.
> *Who's there?*
> Banana split.
> *Banana split who?*
> Banana split, so ice creamed!

Knock-knock.
Who's there?
Barry.
Barry who?
Barry rude of you not to answer the door.

Knock-knock.
Who's there?
Bearskin.
Bearskin who?
Bearskin hibernate in caves all winter.

Knock-knock.
  Who's there?
Bed.
  Bed who?
Bed you can't tell I've
got a code in my nose.

Knock-knock.
  Who's there?
Beehive.
  Beehive who?
Beehive yourself and
get buzzy!

Knock-knock.
  Who's there?
Ben Hur.
  Ben Hur who?
Ben Hur an hour. Let
me in!

Knock-knock.
  Who's there?
Ben and Anna.
  Ben and Anna who?
Ben and Anna split!

Knock-knock.
  Who's there?
Ben and Doris.
  Ben and Doris who?
Ben knocking all
morning—Doris stuck!

Knock-knock.
  Who's there?
Beth.
  Beth who?
Beth wishes on your
birthday, thweetheart.

Knock-knock.
  Who's there?
Bless.
  Bless who?
I don't know—I didn't sneeze.

          Knock-knock.
            Who's there?
          Boysenberry.
            Boysenberry who?
          Boysenberry cute girls are all
          invited to my party.

Knock-knock.
  Who's there?
Butternut.
  Butternut who?
Butternut try
to pick up a skunk.

Knock-knock.
Who's there?
Caesar.
Caesar who?
Caesar great homes for sharks and dolphins.

Knock-knock.
Who's there?
Cameron.
Cameron who?
Cameron film are all you need to take photos.

Knock-knock.
Who's there?
Candice.
Candice who?
Candice class get
any more boring?

Knock-knock.
Who's there?
Cannelloni.
Cannelloni who?
Cannelloni some
money until I get my
allowance?

Knock-knock.
Who's there?
Candidate.
Candidate who?
Candidate be
changed to Friday?

Knock-knock.
Who's there?
Canoe.
Canoe who?
Canoe please get off
my foot?

Knock-knock.
Who's there?
Carmen.
Carmen who?
Carmen get it!
Dinner's ready!

Knock-knock.
Who's there?
Carrie.
Carrie who?
Carrie on with what
you're doing—I'm at
the wrong door.

Knock-knock.
Who's there?
Cash.
Cash who?
Cashew? That's my
favorite nut.

Knock-knock.
Who's there?
Catsup.
Catsup who?
Catsup on the roof.
Should I bring her
down?

Knock-knock.
Who's there?
Cattle.
Cattle who?
Cattle always purr
when you pet it.

Knock-knock.
Who's there?
Cecile.
Cecile who?
Cecile the d-door!
A m-monster's
outs-s-side!

Knock-knock.
Who's there?
Cher.
Cher who?
Cher your toys,
and you'll have lots of friends.

Knock-knock.
Who's there?
Chester.
Chester who?
Chester minute, pardner...
you new in this here town?

Knock-knock.
Who's there?
Cooper.
Cooper who?
Cooper chickens up before they run off!

Knock-knock.
Who's there?
Culver.
Culver who?
Culver up my feet—they're freezing!

Knock-knock.
Who's there?
Dandelion.
Dandelion who?
Dandelion always
growls at Tony the
tiger.

Knock-knock.
Who's there?
Danielle.
Danielle who?
Danielle so loud,
my ears hurt.

Knock-knock.
Who's there?
Daryl.
Daryl who?
Daryl never be anyone
as weird as you.

15

Knock-knock.
Who's there?
Debate.
Debate who?
Debate is what you use to catch de fish.

Knock-knock.
Who's there?
Deceit.
Deceit who?
Deceit of your jeans has a big hole.

Knock-knock.
Who's there?
Deduct.
Deduct who?
Deduct says, "Quack! Quack!"

Knock-knock.
Who's there?
Denise.
Denise who?
Denise are above de
ankles.

Knock-knock.
Who's there?
Dewey.
Dewey who?
Dewey really have to
go to school today?

Knock-knock.
Who's there?
Diana.
Diana who?
Diana thirst...got any
water?

Knock-knock.
Who's there?
Diego.
Diego who?
Diego before de B.

Knock-knock.
Who's there?
Diesel.
Diesel who?
Diesel teach you to fix
your doorbell.

Knock-knock.
  Who's there?
Dinah snores.
  Dinah snores who?
Dinah snores live in Jurassic Park.

Knock-knock.
  Who's there?
Dipsticks.
  Dipsticks who?
Dipsticks on my cracker when I dunk it in the
bowl.

Knock-knock.
Who's there?
Disguise.
Disguise who?
Disguise killing me with all his corny jokes.

Knock-knock.
Who's there?
Dishes.
Dishes who?
Dishes the last time I eat anchovies for breakfast.

Knock-knock.
Who's there?
Dish towel.
Dish towel who?
Dish towel is soaked. Would you get me a dry one?

Knock-knock.
Who's there?
Dismay.
Dismay who?
Dismay not be a good time to knock.

Knock-knock.
Who's there?
Distress.
Distress who?
Distress makes me look like an elephant in a tutu.

Knock-knock.
> *Who's there?*

Doctor Dolittle.
> *Doctor Dolittle who?*

Doctor Dolittle to cure my sore throat.

Knock-knock.
> *Who's there?*

Dogma.
> *Dogma who?*

Dogma best friend.

Knock-knock.
> *Who's there?*

Dumbbell.
> *Dumbbell who?*

Dumbbell doesn't work, so I had to knock.

Knock-knock.
Who's there?
Eclipse.
Eclipse who?
Eclipse his moustache when it curls over his mouth.

Knock-knock.
Who's there?
Egg roll and sausage.
Egg roll and sausage who?
Egg roll off the counter—I never sausage a mess!

Knock-knock.
Who's there?
Eggshell.
Eggshell who?
Eggshell be our breakfast tomorrow morning.

Knock-knock.
Who's there?
Elaine.
Elaine who?
Elaine down on the couch. Should I wake him up?

Knock-knock.
Who's there?
Eliza.
Eliza who?
Eliza lot, but sometimes he tells the truth.

Knock-knock.
Who's there?
Ellie Fence.
Ellie Fence who?
Ellie Fence never forget.

Knock-knock.
Who's there?
Ellis.
Ellis who?
Ellis the letter that comes before M.

Knock-knock.
Who's there?
Emerson.
Emerson who?
Emerson awesome earrings you're wearing.

Knock-knock.
Who's there?
Esau.
Esau who?
Esau a pitbull and jumped back on his bike.

Knock-knock.
Who's there?
Esme.
Esme who?
Esme shirt untucked?

Knock-knock.
Who's there?
Eyedrops.
Eyedrops who?
Eyedrops my keys, then I picks them up.

Knock-knock.
Who's there?
Eyelashes.
Eyelashes who?
Eyelashes myself to the mast
during a storm.

Knock-knock.
Who's there?
Ezra.
Ezra who?
Ezra a doctor in the house?

Knock-knock.
Who's there?
Farrah.
Farrah who?
Farrah way, I saw a
hot air balloon.

Knock-knock.
Who's there?
Fatima.
Fatima who?
Fatima stomach makes
my jeans tight.

Knock-knock.
Who's there?
Felice.
Felice who?
Felice is what sheep
grow on their skin.

25

Knock-knock.
Who's there?
Felix.
Felix who?
Felix my face, that dog is out of here!

Knock-knock.
Who's there?
Fido.
Fido who?
Fido known you were here, I would have phoned.

Knock-knock.
Who's there?
Firewood.
Firewood who?
Firewood sure make these marshmallows melt faster.

Knock-knock.
Who's there?
Flora.
Flora who?
Flora my room sure is a mess!

Knock-knock.
Who's there?
Frieda.
Frieda who?
Frieda cow! She's stuck in the fence!

Knock-knock.
Who's there?
G. I.
G. I. who?
G. I. wish I had a million bucks.

Knock-knock.
Who's there?
Galahad.
Galahad who?
Galahad an ice cream cone, but she
dropped it.

Knock-knock.
   Who's there?
Ghosts go.
   Ghosts go who?
No, silly. Ghosts go "Boo!"

Knock-knock.
   Who's there?
Gladys.
   Gladys who?
Gladys better than feeling sad.

Knock-knock.
   Who's there?
Goblin.
   Goblin who?
Goblin your dinner will give you a
stomach ache.

Knock-knock.
Who's there?
Goliath.
Goliath who?
Goliath down, you
looketh sleepy.

Knock-knock.
Who's there?
Gomez.
Gomez who?
Gomez not allowed to
be chewed in class.

Knock-knock.
Who's there?
Gopher.
Gopher who?
Gopher pizza...I'll wait
here.

Knock-knock.
Who's there?
Greta.
Greta who?
Greta good grade on
that math test and
amaze your parents!

Knock-knock.
Who's there?
Gruesome.
Gruesome who?
Gruesome purple
petunias in my garden.

Knock-knock.
Who's there?
Guest.
Guest who?
Guest wrong, now I'll
have to take the math
test again.

Knock-knock.
Who's there?
Gumby.
Gumby who?
Gumby difficult to
scrape off the bottom
of your shoe.

Knock-knock.
Who's there?
Guru.
Guru who?
Guru two inches last year.

Knock-knock.
Who's there?
Gus.
Gus who?
Gus I'll have to come back later.

Knock-knock.
Who's there?
Gwen.
Gwen who?
Gwen fishing? Can I come?

Knock-knock.
Who's there?
Hairdo.
Hairdo who?
Hairdo a great job of keeping your head warm.

Knock-knock.
Who's there?
Hans.
Hans who?
Hans off my candy bar!

Knock-knock.
Who's there?
Harmony.
Harmony who?
Harmony times have I
asked you to open this
door!

Knock-knock.
Who's there?
Harris.
Harris who?
Harris in my eyes, so
I'd better use some gel.

Knock-knock.
Who's there?
Harry.
Harry who?
Harry up and answer
the door!

Knock-knock.
Who's there?
Harvey.
Harvey who?
Harvey having fun
yet?

Knock-knock.
Who's there?
Hatch-hatch-hatch.
*Hatch-hatch-hatch
who?*
Bless you! Need a
tissue?

Knock-knock.
Who's there?
Hayes.
Hayes who?
Hayes what horses eat.

Knock-knock.
Who's there?
Henrietta.
Henrietta who?
Henrietta healthy lunch.

Knock-knock.
Who's there?
Hobbit.
Hobbit who?
Hobbit your way, smarty-pants.

Knock-knock.
Who's there?
Hogwash.
Hogwash who?
Hogwash in our pool and muddied up the deck.

Knock-knock.
Who's there?
Homer.
Homer who?
Homer away, I always take a bath on Saturday night.

Knock-knock.
Who's there?
Honeycomb.
Honeycomb who?
Honeycomb your hair before we go to the dance.

Knock-knock.
Who's there?
Honeydew.
Honeydew who?
Honeydew you like your pizza hot or cold?

Knock-knock.
> *Who's there?*
Ice cream.
> *Ice cream who?*
Ice cream when I see vampires on TV.

Knock-knock.
> *Who's there?*
Icing.
> *Icing who?*
Icing a song for you on your birthday.

Knock-knock.
Who's there?
Icon.
Icon who?
Icon double-click my mouse faster than you can.

Knock-knock.
Who's there?
Ida.
Ida who?
Ida come earlier, but I crashed my skateboard.

Knock-knock.
Who's there?
Imus.
Imus who?
Imus get out of bed, or I'll be late for school.

Knock-knock.
Who's there?
Income.
Income who?
Income the cats if you leave the door open.

Knock-knock.
Who's there?
Intense.
Intense who?
Intense is where I like
to sleep on camping
trips.

Knock-knock.
Who's there?
Iona.
Iona who?
Iona new skateboard,
nyah, nyah.

Knock-knock.
Who's there?
Iran.
Iran who?
Iran all the way to
second base.

Knock-knock.
Who's there?
Iraq.
Iraq who?
Iraq my brain for
math test answers.

Knock-knock.
Who's there?
Isabel.
Isabel who?
Isabel out of order? I
had to knock.

Knock-knock.
Who's there?
Isadore.
Isadore who?
Isadore open? I'm
freezing!

Knock-knock.
Who's there?
Isaiah.
Isaiah who?
Isaiah little prayer before I go to sleep.

Knock-knock.
Who's there?
Ivana.
Ivana who?
Ivana stick of gum.

Knock-knock.
Who's there?
Izzy.
Izzy who?
Izzy coming now, or isn't he?

Knock-knock.
Who's there?
Jackal.
Jackal who?
Jackal mow your lawn, if you pay him.

Knock-knock.
Who's there?
Jean-Claude.
Jean-Claude who?
Jean-Claude at the dirt as he slid into first base.

Knock-knock.
Who's there?
Jester.
Jester who?
Jester minute...I'm fixing your doorbell.

Knock-knock.
Who's there?
Jody.
Jody who?
Jody first guy to hit a homerun for de team.

Knock-knock.
Who's there?
Josie.
Josie who?
Josie his tent get trashed by a bear!

Knock-knock.
Who's there?
Juan.
Juan who?
Juan day soon I'll be able to drive.

Knock-knock.
Who's there?
Juanita.
Juanita who?
Juanita chocolate-covered ant?

Knock-knock.
Who's there?
Juicy.
Juicy who?
Juicy any ghosts
under my bed?

Knock-knock.
Who's there?
Juliet.
Juliet who?
Juliet birthday cake
at my party.

Knock-knock.
Who's there?
Junior.
Junior who?
Junior flowers come up; July they
bloom.

Knock-knock.
Who's there?
Juno.
Juno who?
Juno what time it is now?

Knock-knock.
Who's there?
Justice.
Justice who?
Justice I thought...your doorbell's broken.

Knock-knock.
Who's there?
Justin.
Justin who?
Justin the neighborhood and thought I'd say
hello.

Knock-knock.
Who's there?
Justina.
Justina who?
Justina nick of time, I caught my pet tarantula
before it escaped.

Knock-knock.
  Who's there?
Kanga.
  Kanga who?
Not kangawho, silly—kangaroo!

Knock-knock.
  Who's there?
Katmandu.
  Katmandu who?
Katmandu exactly what Catwoman do.

Knock-knock.
>Who's there?

Keith.
>Keith who?

Keith me, thweetheart.

Knock-knock.
>Who's there?

Kent.
>Kent who?

Kent go with you, I'm grounded.

Knock-knock.
>Who's there?

Kenya.
>Kenya who?

Kenya see my belly button in these pants?

Knock-knock.
>Who's there?

Kerry.
>Kerry who?

Kerry me over the mud puddle, will you?

Knock-knock.
>Who's there?

Ketchup.
>Ketchup who?

Ketchup to her before she dives into that dumpster!

Knock-knock.
Who's there?
Kiefer.
Kiefer who?
Kiefer my door is lost.

Knock-knock.
Who's there?
Kimmy.
Kimmy who?
Kimmy a little kiss,
Sweetie.

Knock-knock.
Who's there?
Kip.
Kip who?
Kip your sneaky hands
out of my popcorn!

Knock-knock.
Who's there?
Kitty litter.
Kitty litter who?
Kitty litter mouse get
away!

Knock-knock.
Who's there?
Kleenex.
Kleenex who?
Kleenex look nicer than dirty necks.

Knock-knock.
Who's there?
Knotty.
Knotty who?
Knotty little kids get time out.

Knock-knock.
Who's there?
Krakatoa.
Krakatoa who?
Krakatoa on that darn cement step!

Knock-knock.
Who's there?
Lady.
Lady who?
Lady mat on the porch and I won't track mud in the house.

Knock-knock.
Who's there?
Landon.
Landon who?
Landon on your belly hurts!

Knock-knock.
  Who's there?
Leda.
  Leda who?
Leda horse to water but you can't make him drink.

Knock-knock.
  Who's there?
Lena.
  Lena who?
Lena little closer and I'll brush that man-eating spider off your shoulder.

Knock-knock.
  Who's there?
Lettuce and beet.
  Lettuce and beet who?
Lettuce stop this knocking...I'm beet.

Knock-knock.
  Who's there?
Lettuce and turnips.
  Lettuce and turnips who?
Lettuce see if any evidence turnips before we call the cops.

Knock-knock.
  Who's there?
Lewis.
  Lewis who?
Lewis too short to ride the roller coaster.

Knock-knock.
Who's there?
Linda.
Linda who?
Linda hand, please—I can't seem to open this door!

Knock-knock.
Who's there?
Lion.
Lion who?
Lion down for a nap.

Knock-knock.
Who's there?
Lionel.
Lionel who?
Lionel bite if you stick your hand in the cage.

Knock-knock.
Who's there?
Lipstick.
Lipstick who?
Lipstick together when
you blow bubblegum.

Knock-knock.
Who's there?
Lucy.
Lucy who?
Lucy trousers fally
down.

Knock-knock.
Who's there?
Luke.
Luke who?
Luke through the
keyhole and you
might find out.

Knock-knock.
Who's there?
Luther.
Luther who?
Luther jeans would fit
me much better.

Knock-knock.
Who's there?
Lydia.
Lydia who?
Lydia teapot is
cracked.

M

Knock-knock.
> *Who's there?*

Macaw.
> *Macaw who?*

Macaw won't start. Can you give me a lift?

> Knock-knock.
>> *Who's there?*
>
> Mackie.
>> *Mackie who?*
>
> Mackie roni and cheese.

Knock-knock.
Who's there?
Major.
Major who?
Major answer the door, didn't I?

Knock-knock.
Who's there?
Mandissa.
Mandissa who?
Mandissa great place for a picnic.

Knock-knock.
Who's there?
Mandy.
Mandy who?
Mandy lifeboats—we've hit an iceberg!

Knock-knock.
> *Who's there?*

Marcus.
> *Marcus who?*

Marcus down for two
tickets, please.

Knock-knock.
> *Who's there?*

Marmalade.
> *Marmalade who?*

Marmalade an egg.

Knock-knock.
> *Who's there?*

Maura.
> *Maura who?*

Maura those French fries
and another burger, please.

Knock-knock.
> *Who's there?*

Maya.
> *Maya who?*

Maya good joke teller?

Knock-knock.
> *Who's there?*

Meat patty.
> *Meat patty who?*

Meat Patty, then meet
her brother Frank Furter.

Knock-knock.
   Who's there?
Mia.
   Mia who?
Mia genius; you a
dummy.

Knock-knock.
   Who's there?
Moira.
   Moira who?
Moira that birthday
cake, please.

Knock-knock.
   Who's there?
Momma.
   Momma who?
Momma good cook.

Knock-knock.
   Who's there?
Musket.
   Musket who?
Musket a job—I'm
broke.

Knock-knock.
   Who's there?
Myth.
   Myth who?
Myth my two fwont
teefth in my mowfth.

Knock-knock.
Who's there?
Nadia.
Nadia who?
Nadia head if you understand the question.

   Knock-knock.
   Who's there?
   Nanny.
   Nanny who?
   Nanny one going to answer this door?

Knock-knock.
Who's there?
Nantucket.
Nantucket who?
Nantucket, but she'll
give it right back.

Knock-knock.
Who's there?
Napkin.
Napkin who?
Napkin pep you up if
you don't snooze too
long.

Knock-knock.
Who's there?
Needle.
Needle who?
Needle little sympathy.

Knock-knock.
Who's there?
Nickel.
Nickel who?
Nickel dance the hula
if we buy him a grass
skirt.

Knock-knock.
Who's there?
Noah.
Noah who?
Noah good place to find more jokes?

Knock-knock.
Who's there?
Noggin.
Noggin who?
Noggin on your door for about an hour now.

Knock-knock.
Who's there?
Nonna.
Nonna who?
Nonna your business who I am.

Knock-knock.
Who's there?
Norma Lee.
Norma Lee who?
Norma Lee I rinse my mouth
after the dog kisses me.

Knock-knock.
Who's there?
Norway.
Norway who?
Norway am I going to
open this door.

Knock-knock.
Who's there?
Nosey.
Nosey who?
Nosey can't get in,
so he's going to get a key.

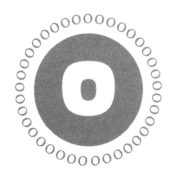

Knock-knock.
Who's there?
Oil.
Oil who?
Oil see you later, alligator.

Knock-knock.
Who's there?
Oink-oink.
Oink-oink who?
Make up your mind...are you a pig or an owl?

Knock-knock.
Who's there?
Olaf.
Olaf who?
Olaf if you tickle my feet.

Knock-knock.
Who's there?
Olive.
Olive who?
Olive on Maple Street. Where do you live?

Knock-knock.
Who's there?
Oliver.
Oliver who?
Oliver clothes got wet when she
fell into the pool.

Knock-knock.
Who's there?
Ollie.
Ollie who?
Ollie your teeth are green!
Don't you brush?

Knock-knock.
Who's there?
Oman.
Oman who?
Oman, are you cute!

Knock-knock.
Who's there?
Omelet and butter.
Omelet and butter who?
Omelet stronger than I look, so
you butter watch out.

Knock-knock.
Who's there?
Osborn.
Osborn who?
Osborn in a hospital.
Where's you born?

Knock-knock.
Who's there?
Oslo.
Oslo who?
Oslo down for squirrels.

Knock-knock.
Who's there?
Oswald.
Oswald who?
Oswald my bubblegum!

Knock-knock.
Who's there?
Owl.
Owl who?
Owl tell you a secret if you don't blab it around.

Knock-knock.
Who's there?
Oz.
Oz who?
Oz got to sneeze! Stand back!

Knock-knock.
Who's there?
Ozzie.
Ozzie who?
Ozzie you when you get back.

Knock-knock.
  Who's there?
Panther.
  Panther who?
Panther no panth, I'm going thwimming.

Knock-knock.
  Who's there?
Paradise.
  Paradise who?
Paradise are all you need to play board games.

Knock-knock.
Who's there?
Pecan.
Pecan who?
Pecan somebody your own size!

Knock-knock.
Who's there?
Peeka.
Peeka who?
Not peeka who, silly...peekaboo.

Knock-knock.
Who's there?
Phyllis.
Phyllis who?
Phyllis in on the latest gossip.

Knock-knock.
Who's there?
Pickle.
Pickle who?
Pickle work better than a shovel
in your garden.

Knock-knock.
Who's there?
Piggyback.
Piggyback who?
Piggyback home before
the Big Bad Wolf
could catch it.

Knock-knock.
Who's there?
Pink panther.
Pink panther who?
Pink panther more
girlish than blue
panth.

Knock-knock.
Who's there?
Pizza.
Pizza who?
Pizza nice guy when
you get to know him.

Knock-knock.
Who's there?
Plato.
Plato who?
Plato nachos, please.

Knock-knock.
Who's there?
Police.
Police who?
Police let me in!
There's a hurricane
out here!

Knock-knock.
Who's there?
Poodle.
Poodle who?
Poodle little chow in
Fido's dish, will you?

Knock-knock.
Who's there?
Popcan.
Popcan who?
Popcan make you
burp if you drink it
too fast.

Knock-knock.
Who's there?
Pudding.
Pudding who?
Pudding your hand in
a crocodile's mouth is
really dumb.

Knock-knock.
Who's there?
Punch.
Punch who?
Not me!

Knock-knock.
Who's there?
Q-T.
Q-T who?
Q-T pie, you're adorable.

Knock-knock.
Who's there?
Q-tip.
Q-tip who?
Q-tip over when you do a handstand?

Knock-knock.
Who's there?
Quacker.
Quacker who?
Quacker cwumbs are in my bed.

Knock-knock.
Who's there?
Quacks.
Quacks who?
Quacks in the ground come
from earthquacks.

Knock-knock.
Who's there?
Queen.
Queen who?
Queen up your room, please.

Knock-knock.
Who's there?
Queue.
Queue who?
Queue better floss that spinach
out of your teeth.

Knock-knock.
Who's there?
Raisin.
Raisin who?
Raisin chickens is a cheep-cheep job.

Knock-knock.
Who's there?
Razor.
Razor who?
Razor hand if you have the correct answer.

Knock-knock.
Who's there?
Ringo.
Ringo who?
Ringo on the bride's finger.

Knock-knock.
Who's there?
Robin.
Robin who?
Robin the cookie jar again?

Knock-knock.
Who's there?
Rocco.
Rocco who?
Rocco-bye baby, on the treetop....

Knock-knock.
Who's there?
Ron.
Ron who?
Ron faster! There's a tyrannosaurus after us!

Knock-knock.
Who's there?
Sadie.
Sadie who?
Sadie magic word, and I'll pass the nuts.

Knock-knock.
Who's there?
Salmon and porpoise.
Salmon and porpoise who?
Salmon Alex swam with a dolphin,
but they didn't do it on porpoise.

Knock-knock.
Who's there?
Samoa.
Samoa who?
Samoa that super-sized soda will give me the hiccups.

Knock-knock.
Who's there?
Sasha.
Sasha who?
Sasha lot of silly questions!

Knock-knock.
Who's there?
Santa.
Santa who?
Santa e-mail to you but you never replied.

Knock-knock.
Who's there?
Selma.
Selma who?
Selma bike, then I'll buy a scooter.

Knock-knock.
Who's there?
Senior.
Senior who?
Senior boa constrictor around here lately?

Knock-knock.
Who's there?
Sharon.
Sharon who?
Sharon my pizza is not what I had in mind.

Knock-knock.
Who's there?
Sherwood.
Sherwood who?
Sherwood be more fun if my skateboard had wheels.

Knock-knock.
Who's there?
Shirley.
Shirley who?
Shirley you must know where I left my homework.

Knock-knock.
  Who's there?
Sid.
  Sid who?
Sid down and speak up.

Knock-knock.
  Who's there?
Ski tow.
  Ski tow who?
Ski tow bites itch like crazy.

Knock-knock.
  Who's there?
Snow.
  Snow who?
Snow body but me knows who Santa really is.

Knock-knock.
  Who's there?
Sonia.
  Sonia who?
Sonia matter of time before I turn into a werewolf.

Knock-knock.
  Who's there?
Spell.
  Spell who?
W-H-O.

Knock-knock.
  Who's there?
Statue.
  Statue who?
Statue who burped just now?

Knock-knock.
  Who's there?
Talia.
  Talia who?
Talia a bedtime story if you put your jammies on.

Knock-knock.
  Who's there?
Tamara.
  Tamara who?
Tamara is Saturday; today is Friday.

Knock-knock.
Who's there?
Tara.
Tara who?
Tara hole in your T-shirt?

Knock-knock.
Who's there?
Tarzan.
Tarzan who?
Tarzan stripes decorate flags of many nations.

Knock-knock.
Who's there?
Teddy bear.
Teddy bear who?
Teddy bear because he's taking a bath.

Knock-knock.
Who's there?
Knock-knock.
Who's there?
Thesis.
Thesis who?
Thesis the last time
I'm knocking!

Knock-knock.
Who's there?
Thumb.
Thumb who?
Thumb like it hot,
thumb like it cold.

Knock-knock.
Who's there?
Thistle.
Thistle who?
Thistle be me—
who are you?

Knock-knock.
Who's there?
Thumping.
Thumping who?
Thumping gooey is
dripping down your
chin.

Knock-knock.
Who's there?
Throat.
Throat who?
Throat to me, and I'll
score a touchdown.

Knock-knock.
Who's there?
Tilda.
Tilda who?
Tilda sun rises, I'll be
doing my homework.

Knock-knock.
Who's there?
Tom Sawyer.
Tom Sawyer who?
Tom Sawyer underwear in gym class.

Knock-knock.
Who's there?
Tooth.
Tooth who?
Tooth company, threeth a crowd.

Knock-knock.
Who's there?
Tuba.
Tuba who?
Tuba toothpaste makes my teeth sparkle.

Knock-knock.
Who's there?
Tulips.
Tulips who?
Tulips kiss better than one lip.

Knock-knock.
Who's there?
U-2.
U-2 who?
U-2 can be a rock star in ten easy lessons!

Knock-knock.
Who's there?
U-4.
U-4 who?
U-4 me, and me for you.

Knock-knock.
Who's there?
Ubangi.
Ubangi who?
Ubangi on my door
one more time and
you're history!

Knock-knock.
Who's there?
UCI.
UCI who?
UCI had to knock
because your doorbell
doesn't work.

Knock-knock.
Who's there?
Udder.
Udder who?
Udder joke's better
than this one.

Knock-knock.
Who's there?
Uganda.
Uganda who?
Uganda lot of weight
over vacation.

Knock-knock.
Who's there?
Uma.
Uma who?
Uma good buddy.

Knock-knock.
Who's there?
Unaware.
Unaware who?
Unaware sticking
out of your jeans!

Knock-knock.
Who's there?
Unit.
Unit who?
Unit me a sweater,
and I'll knit you
some mittens.

Knock-knock.
Who's there?
Urchin.
Urchin who?
Urchin sticks out
below her teeth.

Knock-knock.
Who's there?
Uriah.
Uriah who?
Uriah looks bloodshot.

Knock-knock.
Who's there?
Uruguay.
Uruguay who?
Uruguay who knows how to treat a gwirl.

Knock-knock.
Who's there?
Usher.
Usher who?
Usher up...she's singing too loud.

Knock-knock.
  Who's there?
Vanessa.
  Vanessa who?
Vanessa bus coming?

      Knock-knock.
        Who's there?
      Venice.
        Venice who?
      Venice your next birthday?

Knock-knock.
  Who's there?
Vera.
  Vera who?
Vera interesting...can you repeat that?

    Knock-knock.
      Who's there?
    Viper.
      Viper who?
    Viper nose before it drips on her T-shirt.

Knock-knock.
  Who's there?
Vlad.
  Vlad who?
Vlad to meet you, Count Dracula.

    Knock-knock.
      Who's there?
    Voodoo.
      Voodoo who?
    Voodoo you think you're kidding?

Knock-knock.
  Who's there?
W.
  W who?
W, and your clone can answer the door!

Knock-knock.
  Who's there?
Waddle.
  Waddle who?
Waddle you do if I knock again?

Knock-knock.
Who's there?
Wayne.
Wayne who?
Wayne is falling on
my pawade.

Knock-knock.
Who's there?
Wes.
Wes who?
Wes the exit? I'm lost!

Knock-knock.
Who's there?
Weasel.
Weasel who?
Weasel for your dog,
and maybe she'll come
home.

Knock-knock.
Who's there?
Whale.
Whale who?
Whale I'll be a
monkey's uncle!

Knock-knock.
Who's there?
Wendy.
Wendy who?
Wendy moon comes
up, de sun goes down.

Knock-knock.
Who's there?
Who.
Who who?
Do you hear an owl
around here?

Knock-knock.
  Who's there?
Why do owls go.
  Why do owls go who?
Because that's how they talk, silly!

Knock-knock.
  Who's there?
Wiggle.
  Wiggle who?
Wiggle fall off your head if the wind blows hard.

Knock-knock.
  Who's there?
Wire.
  Wire who?
Wire you asking? It's me, knucklehead.

Knock-knock.
Who's there?
Witches.
Witches who?
Witches the one you want? This one or that?

    Knock-knock.
      Who's there?
    Wooden shoe.
      Wooden shoe who?
    Wooden shoe like to sleep over?

Knock-knock.
Who's there?
Wonton.
Wonton who?
Wonton more pizza than you can eat is a waste
of food.

    Knock-knock.
      Who's there?
    Woodchuck.
      Woodchuck who?
    Woodchuck mow the lawn if we paid him?

Knock-knock.
   Who's there?
X.
   X who?
X and bacon are my favorite breakfast foods.

Knock-knock.
   Who's there?
XL.
   XL who?
XL at sports and you'll be famous.

Knock-knock.
Who's there?
Xavier.
Xavier who?
Xavier ticket stubs and win a prize!

Knock-knock.
Who's there?
Xenia.
Xenia who?
Xenia at the mall, but you didn't see me.

Knock-knock.
Who's there?
Xerox.
Xerox who?
Xerox fell on my head when I went mountain climbing.

Knock-knock.
Who's there?
Xs.
Xs who?
Xs are used by lumberjacks to cut down trees.

Knock-knock.
Who's there?
Yaw.
Yaw who?
Giddyap! Ride 'em, cowboy!

Knock-knock.
Who's there?
Yoda.
Yoda who?
Yoda man.

Knock-knock.
Who's there?
Yolanda.
Yolanda who?
Yolanda plane on the runway.

Knock-knock.
Who's there?
Yoo.
Yoo who?
Yoo-hoo, yourself.

Knock-knock.
Who's there?
Yukon.
Yukon who?
Yukon come with us if you pay your share.

> Knock-knock.
> *Who's there?*
> Yule.
> *Yule who?*
> Yule be sorry if you miss Santa.

Knock-knock.
Who's there?
Yuma.
Yuma who?
Yuma very best friend.

> Knock-knock.
> *Who's there?*
> Yvonne.
> *Yvonne who?*
> Yvonne my own mother doesn't
> recognize me with this wig on.

Knock-knock.
Who's there?
Zany.
Zany who?
Zany body home?

Knock-knock.
Who's there?
Zelda.
Zelda who?
Zelda bike to my neighbor.

Knock-knock.
Who's there?
Zenia.
Zenia who?
Zenia citizens get in
for half price.

Knock-knock.
Who's there?
Zeno.
Zeno who?
Zeno evil, hear no evil,
speak no evil.

Knock-knock.
Who's there?
Zeus.
Zeus who?
Zeus are where wild
animals are caged.

Knock-knock.
Who's there?
Zing.
Zing who?
Zing zome zongs with
me, okay?

Knock-knock.
Who's there?
Zoom.
Zoom who?
Zoom did you expect?

Knock-knock.
Who's there?
Zounds.
Zounds who?
Zounds! Zounds like this
might be the last joke.
It is!

index index index **Index** index index index